Homemade Organic Body Wash for Your Kids: Give Your Kids' Skin a Lift with these 30 Homemade Kiddie Organic Body Washes

Ida Smith

Published by Ida Smith, 2021.

HOMEMADE ORGANIC BODY WASH FOR YOUR KIDS: GIVE YOUR KIDS' SKIN A LIFT WITH THESE 30 HOMEMADE KIDDIE ORGANIC BODY WASHES

First edition. September 19, 2021.

ISBN: 979-8201038069

Written by Ida Smith.

Table of Contents

Introduction

There are 2 challenges that parents have with commercial kiddie skincare products; they either contain toxic ingredients, or they are unnecessarily on the high price.

When parents face these challenges, they begin to fret about how to take care of their kids' skin.

I have the perfect answer for you; this book is all that you need!

The recipes in the book don't only contain organic and safe ingredients, but they cost next to nothing to prepare!!

So, looking for how to keep the playful mini you squeaky clean, refreshed, rejuvenated, and fresh? Get this book now!!!

Recipe 1 - Olive and Lemon Body Wash

This body wash will help to remove deep grime and dirt from your kids' skin, to reveal moisturized, smooth, and revived skin!

Prep time: 04 minutes
Cooking time: nil
Servings: 1 container
Ingredients

- 7 tablespoons liquid castile soap
- 50 tablespoons lemon oil
- 2 tablespoons olive oil
- 1 tablespoon vegetable glycerin
- 1 tablespoon honey

Directions

Mix everything in a bowl.
Pour in a body wash bottle.

Recipe 2 - Grapeseed and Vanilla Body Wash

You and your kids don't have to worry about scars and damaged skin!! Because this body wash will help to improve, repair, and regenerate them!!

Prep time: 06 minutes
Cooking time: nil
Servings: 1 container
Ingredients

- 4 tablespoons grapeseed oil
- 4 tablespoons distilled water
- 1 tablespoon milk
- 60 drops vanilla oil
- 1 tablespoon vegetable glycerin
- 12 tablespoons liquid castile soap
- 1 tablespoon honey

Directions

Toss everything well in a bowl.

Pour into your body wash bottle

Recipe 3 - Jojoba and Lemon Body Wash

This body wash doesn't coat your kids' skin like store bought kiddie body washes might do. Instead, it leaves your kids' skin looking smooth and flawless!

Prep time: 07 minutes

Cooking time: nil

Servings: 1 container

Ingredients

- 50 drops lemon oil
- 3 tablespoons jojoba oil
- 1 tablespoon honey
- 6 tablespoons liquid castile soap
- 1 tablespoon vegetable glycerin

Directions

Combine all 5 ingredients in a bowl. Mix well. Transfer to your body wash bottle.

Recipe 4 - Oregano and Avocado Body Wash

This lightly scented body wash helps mitigate bacterial growth and eliminate unwanted odors from your kids' bodies, leaving them smelling like fresh sunlight!!

Prep time: 07 minutes

Cooking time: nil

Servings: 1 container

Ingredients

- 50g oregano oil
- 1 teaspoon vitamin E oil
- 1 tablespoon avocado oil
- 11 tablespoons liquid castile soap
- 1 tablespoon honey

Directions

Combine everything in a bowl.

Mix well.

Transfer to your body wash bottle.

Recipe 5 - Coconut and Vetiver Body Wash

With its subtle sweet aroma, this body wash is good for your kids in summer!

Prep time: 06 minutes
Cooking time: nil
Servings: 2 containers
Ingredients

- 50 drops vetiver oil
- 1 tablespoon coconut oil
- 1 tablespoon honey
- 9 tablespoons liquid castile soap
- 1 tablespoon vegetable glycerin

Directions
Combine everything in a jar.
Mix well.

Transfer to your body wash bottle.

Recipe 6 - Grapeseed and Lavender Body Wash

With the calming effect and aroma of lavender coupled with the skin hydrating feature of grapeseed oil, your kids' skin will never remain the same again!!!

Prep time: 10 minutes
Cooking time: nil
Servings: 1 container
Ingredients

- 10 tablespoons liquid castile soap
- 25 drops lavender oil
- 2 tablespoons grapeseed oil
- 5 tablespoons honey
- 2 tablespoons vegetable glycerin

Directions

Combine the 5 ingredients in a bowl

Mix well.

Transfer to a container with a pump.

You're good to go!!

Recipe 7 - Black Seed and Frankincense Body Wash

The soothing and calm effect of this body wash will make your kid want to take his or her bath always!!

Prep time: 05 minutes

Cooking time: nil

Servings: 1 container

INGREDIENTS

- 65 drops frankincense oil
- 4 teaspoons black seed oil
- 2 tablespoons honey
- 13 tablespoons liquid castile soap
- 2 teaspoons vegetable glycerin
- 3 tablespoons distilled water

Directions
Combine all in a bowl.
Pour in your body wash bottle.

Recipe 8 - Vanilla and Avocado Body Wash

This sultry and creamy vanilla and avocado body wash will pamper your kids' skin and thrill their senses.

Prep time: 05 minutes

Cooking time: nil

Servings: 1 container

Ingredients

- 40g vanilla oil
- 60g liquid body wash
- 55g distilled water
- 5g avocado oil
- 5g vegetable glycerin

Directions

Throw in everything in a bowl. Stir well to combine everything.

Transfer to your body wash container.

That's all.

Recipe 9 - Sweet Almond and Oregano Body Wash

This body wash will help to improve your kids' complexion, balance skin moisture, and heal sun damage!!

Prep time: 07 minutes

Cooking time: nil

Servings: 1 container

Ingredients

- 53 drops oregano oil
- 2 tablespoons sweet almond oil
- 1 tablespoon vegetable glycerin
- 1 tablespoon honey
- 2 tablespoons distilled water
- 1 tablespoon milk
- 10 tablespoons liquid castile soap

Directions
Combine all in a jar.
Mix well.
Transfer to your clean body wash bottle.

Recipe 10 - Jojoba and Hyssop Body Wash

The sacredness of hyssop oil is not the only reason why this baby oil is the best thing for your kids' skin. The aroma-therapeutic property of it and its ability to treat colds, infections, asthma, and skin reactions are good reasons to make it your choice.

Coupled with the refreshing and rejuvenating properties of jojoba oil, your kids' bodies will be kept refreshed and his/her senses heightened!

Prep time: 04 minutes
Cooking time: nil
Servings: 1 container
Ingredients

- 60 drops hyssop oil
- 10 tablespoons liquid castile soap
- 1 tablespoon jojoba oil

- 1 tablespoon vegetable glycerin
- 3 tablespoons honey
- 1 dash vitamin E oil

Directions

Throw in everything in a bowl.

Mix well.

Transfer to your body wash bottle.

Recipe 11 - Apricot Kernel and Ylang Ylang Body Wash

This body wash will leave your kids' skin toned, supple, and silky!!

Prep time: 05 minutes

Cooking time: nil

Servings: 1 container

Ingredients

- 60 drops ylang yang oil
- 2 tablespoons apricot kernel oil
- 1 tablespoon vegetable glycerin
- 8 tablespoons liquid castile soap
- 1 tablespoon vitamin E oil

Directions

Mix everything in a bowl.

Pour in a bottle.

Recipe 12 - Frankincense and Rosehip Body Wash

This body wash doesn't only cleanse your kids' bodies, but it also soothes their skin and balances oil production in their skin!!

Prep time: 07 minutes
Cooking time: nil
Servings: 1 container
Ingredients

- 600g frankincense oil
- 70g coconut oil
- 20g rosehip oil
- 200g distilled water
- 300g liquid castile soap

Directions
Dump all your ingredients in a jar.

Shake well to get the ingredients well mixed.
Keep aside for 24 hours.
Transfer to a body wash pump container.

Recipe 13 - Rosehip and Grapefruit Body Wash

Have your kid feeling refreshed and ready to save the world with this scented body wash!

Prep time: 05 minutes
Cooking time: nil
Servings: 1 container
Ingredients

- 57 drops grapefruit oil
- 1 tablespoon rosehip oil
- 1 tablespoon honey
- 9 tablespoons liquid castile soap
- 1 tablespoon vitamin E

Directions

Mix all ingredients in a jar.
Stir well.
Transfer to a pump container

Recipe 14 - Coconut and Lemon Body Wash

Ensuring that your kids' skin retains its color and tone is not an easy thing. But with the help of this body wash, be rest assured that your kids' skin will be well toned and exfoliated.

Prep time: 10 minutes
Cooking time: nil
Servings: 2 containers
Ingredients

- 180g coconut oil
- 1500g lemon oil
- 60g jojoba oil
- 600g distilled water
- 250g glycerin soap

Directions

Mix all your 5 ingredients in a bowl.

Combine well.

Transfer to 2 clean body wash containers.

Recipe 15 - Grapeseed and Lemon Body Wash

This body wash will help relax, firm, smoothen, and soften your kids' skin without any stickiness!

Prep time: 06 minutes
Cooking time: nil
Servings: 1 container
Ingredients

- 54 drops lemon oil
- 2 tablespoons grapeseed oil
- 1 tablespoon honey
- 10 tablespoons liquid castile soap
- 1 tablespoon vegetable glycerin

Directions

Throw in all you have in a bowl. Stir well.
Pour in a container.

Recipe 16 - Lavender and Sweet Almond Body Wash

Are your kids the type that gets dirty from playing all day? Not to worry, this sweet almond and lavender kiddie body wash will wash away all impurities and also rejuvenate your kids' skin.

Prep time: 06 minutes

Cooking time: nil

Servings: 1 container

Ingredients

- 50 drops lavender oil
- 3 teaspoons sweet almond oil
- 10 tablespoons coconut liquid soap
- 1 tablespoon vitamin E
- 1 teaspoon vegetable glycerin

Directions

Combine all in a bowl. Mix well.
Transfer to a container.

Recipe 17 - Argan and Eucalyptus Body Wash

This excellent detoxifying body wash helps wash away your kids' dull skin to reveal a soft, refined, smooth, and bright skin tone!!

Prep time: 05 minutes
Cooking time: nil
Servings: 1 container
Ingredients

- 60 drops eucalyptus oil
- 2 tablespoons argan oil
- 11 tablespoons liquid castile soap
- 1 tablespoon honey
- 1 tablespoon vegetable glycerin

Directions

Combine all in a bowl.
Mix well.
Pour in a body wash bottle.

Recipe 18 - Grapeseed and Chamomile Body Wash

Kids are the worse when it comes to injuries. Engaging in some outdoor and indoor activities makes them susceptible to injuries, and as such you spend days trying to get the wounds to heal up!

Bathing your injured kids with this body wash will not only moisturize the skin and keep it safe from bacteria but also help heal the scars very fast!!

Prep time: 08 minutes

Cooking time: nil

Servings: 2 ounces

Ingredients

- 2 drops vitamin E
- 3 tablespoons liquid castile soap
- 10 tablespoons grapeseed oil
- 6 drops lavender oil
- 3 tablespoons cold brewed chamomile tea

Directions
Combine everything in a bowl.
Mix well. Set aside for a while.
Pour into your clean body wash bottle.

Recipe 19 - Rosehip and Myrrh Body Wash

Asides from smoothening your kids' skin, this body wash moisturizes, cleans, and tightens the skin to mitigate cracking and chapping of skin.

Prep time: 06 minutes

Cooking time: nil

Servings: 1 container

INGREDIENTS

- 53 drops myrrh oil
- 9 tablespoons liquid castile soap
- 3 teaspoons rosehip oil
- 1 tablespoon vitamin E
- 1 tablespoon liquid milk
- 1 tablespoon vegetable glycerin

Directions
Combine all in a bowl. Stir well.
Pour in your body wash bottle.

Recipe 20 - Rosehip and Cedar Wood Body Wash

Saying this body wash is an all round body wash is no gainsaying. It has a lot of benefits such as moisturizing and hydrating your kids' skin.

Also, the body wash helps repel insects, relieve cough, improve sleep, relieve itchy scalp, heal wounds, and treat oily skin.

Prep time: 07 minutes

Cooking time: nil

Servings: 1 container

Ingredients

- 2 teaspoons rosehip oil
- 60 drops cedar wood oil
- 1 tablespoon vitamin E oil
- 9 tablespoons liquid castile soap

- 1 tablespoon honey

Directions

Combine everything in a bowl. Stir well.
Pour in your clean body wash container.

Recipe 21 - Spearmint and Rosehip Body Wash

Nourishing, protecting, and soothing are all that this body wash does!!!

Prep time: 06 minutes
Cooking time: nil
Servings: 1 container
Ingredients

- 50 drops spearmint oil
- 1 tablespoon vitamin E oil
- 2 tablespoons rosehip oil
- 10 tablespoons liquid castile soap
- 1 tablespoon honey

Directions

Mix all in a bowl.

Pour in your body wash bottle.

Recipe 22 - Jojoba and Vanilla Body Wash

With everyday use, this body wash helps retain the moisture of your kids' skin, leaving his or her skin feeling soft, supple, and smooth.

Prep time: 05 minutes
Cooking time: nil
Servings: 1 container
Ingredients

- 3 teaspoons jojoba oil
- 12 tablespoons liquid castile soap
- 1 tablespoon vitamin E
- 1 tablespoon honey
- 55 drops vanilla oil

Directions

Combine everything in a jar. Toss to be well combined. Transfer to your body wash bottle.

Recipe 23 - Avocado and Vetiver Body Wash

Known as "Oil of Tranquility," combining vetiver oil and avocado oil helps to stimulate your kids' muscles and bones into a state of calmness.

Prep time: 05 minutes
Cooking time: nil
Servings: 1 container
Ingredients

- 2 drops vitamin E oil
- 2 tablespoons liquid castile soap
- 8 drops vetiver oil
- 3 tablespoons avocado oil
- 1 tablespoon honey

Directions
Combine all in a jar.
Mix well.
Pour in a body wash bottle.

Recipe 24 - Apricot and Peppermint Body Wash

The perfect combination of apricot kernel oil and peppermint helps soothe and calm your kids' senses and bodies too!!

Prep time: 05 minutes
Cooking time: nil
Servings: 1 container
Ingredients

- 45 drops peppermint oil
- 2 teaspoons apricot oil
- 1 teaspoon honey
- 7 tablespoons liquid castile soap
- 1 teaspoon vitamin E oil

Directions

Mix everything in a jar.

Transfer to your liquid body wash bottle.

Recipe 25 - Sunflower and Oregano Body Wash

This body wash deeply cleans, nourishes, soothes, and rejuvenates your kids' skin, leaving them feeling and looking clean and fresh always.

Prep time: 06 minutes
Cooking time: nil
Servings: 2 containers
Ingredients

- 92 drops oregano oil
- 4 tablespoons sunflower oil
- 50g distilled water
- 2 tablespoons honey
- 1 cup liquid castile soap

- 2 tablespoons vitamin E
- 2 tablespoons vegetable glycerin

Directions

Throw in all in a bowl.

Mix well.

Pour in 2 body wash bottles.

Recipe 26 - Sweet Almond, Honey, and Orange Body Wash

Asides from the antioxidant, antibacterial, and antifungal properties of this body wash, the scent has a calming and relaxing effect on your kids!!

Prep time: 04 minutes
Cooking time: nil
Servings: 1 container
Ingredients

- 1 tablespoon sweet almond oil
- 8 tablespoons castile soap
- 1 dash vitamin E
- 3 tablespoons honey
- 45 drops orange oil
- 1 teaspoon vegetable glycerin

Directions

Throw everything in a jar. Stir to mix well.
Transfer to your clean body wash bottle.

Recipe 27 - Argan and Hyssop Body Wash

Did your kids have a rough day at school? Not to worry!!! This body wash will have their bodies clean and spirits lifted in no time!!

Prep time: 05 minutes

Cooking time: nil

Servings: 1 container

Ingredients

- 60 drops hyssop oil
- 3 teaspoons argan oil
- 1 tablespoon vegetable glycerin
- 10 tablespoons liquid castile soap
- 1 tablespoon vitamin E oil
- 1 tablespoon honey

Directions

Combine everything in a body wash bottle.

Shake well.

Start washing.

Recipe 28 - Lavender and Olive Body Wash

This buttery and soft body wash leaves your kids' bodies smooth and fresh!

Prep time: 05 minutes
Cooking time: nil
Servings: 1 container
Ingredients

- 40 drops lavender oil
- 4 tablespoons olive oil
- 4 tablespoons liquid castile soap
- 3 tablespoons honey
- 2 teaspoons vegetable glycerin

Directions

Mix the 5 ingredients well in a jar.
Transfer to your body wash bottle.

Recipe 29 - Black Seed and Rose Body Wash

This combo fades discoloration and mitigates skin reactions.

Prep time: 06 minutes
Cooking time: nil
Servings: 1 container
Ingredients

- 40 drops rose oil
- 5 tablespoons black seed oil
- 1 teaspoon honey
- 4 tablespoons liquid castile soap
- 1 tablespoon vegetable glycerin

Directions

Combine all in a body wash bottle. Shake well.

Recipe 30 - Rosehip and Eucalyptus Body Wash

A beautiful well scented bottle full of body wash that exfoliates and restores skin balance and uplifts your kids' bodies and minds, this body wash is everything that your kids need to look, feel, and smell well!!

Prep time: 06 minutes
Cooking time: nil
Servings: 2 containers
Ingredients

- 100 drops eucalyptus oil
- 10 tablespoons rosehip oil
- 10 tablespoons liquid castile soap
- 4 tablespoons vegetable glycerin
- 4 tablespoons honey

Directions

Combine everything in a bowl.

Mix well.

Divide into 2 clean body wash bottles.

Conclusion

Store bought kiddie body wash contains lots of artificial ingredients that can irritate and destroy your kids' skin, and we say no to that!

Rather than rely on store bought artificially made kiddie body wash for our kids' skin, let's decide to take the onus on ourselves to be the ones to prepare what body wash our kids will use.

To help achieve this, I strongly hope that this book will do justice to that!!!

Don't miss out!

Visit the website below and you can sign up to receive emails whenever Ida Smith publishes a new book. There's no charge and no obligation.

https://books2read.com/r/B-A-LRXL-YXASB

BOOKS 2 READ

Connecting independent readers to independent writers.

www.ingramcontent.com/pod-product-compliance
Ingram Content Group UK Ltd.
Pitfield, Milton Keynes, MK11 3LW, UK
UKHW061655190726
13853UKWH00008B/2216